God Is Forever

by Sherry Small Sundick

Illustrations by Edna Searles

Publisher, Sherry Small Sundick, Potomac, MD

© Copyright Sherry Small Sundick 2009

Library of Congress Catalog Card Number: 2009906242
ISBN: 0-9745986-2-3

First Edition: Large Print

Printed by Mark Divita T/A PRINTMARK, Rockville, MD
Email: printmark.md@gmail.com

Dedication

God Is Forever
is dedicated to my daughters:

Suzy Balamaci
and
Amy Bruce

About the Author

This is Sherry Small Sundick's fourteenth book. A freelance writer and poet, she resides in Potomac, Maryland. Sherry has published articles and poems in local and national newspapers, magazines and literary journals including *The Northwest Current, The Wheaton News, The Washington Post, Maryland Magazine, Wellspring, The Archer, The Poet, Offerings, I WILL SING THY PRAISES, BROKEN STREETS IV, Modus Operandi and Cardinal Poetry Review.*

About the Illustrator

This is Edna Searles' tenth book of illustrations. A resident of Clarksburg, Maryland, she has shown artwork locally and nationally with many one-person exhibits including the Virginia Corporate Exhibits of Contel and GTE and the Arnot Art Museum in New York. Her works are in the permanent collections of Montgomery County, Maryland and the Gwinnett Fine Arts Center in Georgia and numerous private collections around the world.

For further information, email Edna Searles at artistpalette@aol.com.

Contents

Contents

God Is Forever

Godly World of Wonders

Butterfly clouds in

blueberry skies.

Emerald forests filled

with honeysuckle.

Horses dancing

in meadows.

The innocence of childhood

a baby's smile

the compassion

of humanity.

Midnight

Midnight— the hour of

deepest thought.

Time to prepare

for tomorrow's

travails and

surprises.

Midnight—

most peaceful—

people sleeping

in a quiet house

except for soothing rain

on rooftops.

Maine Woods

Blueberry-picking

in pine-scented forests.

Bareback-riding along

verdant trails.

Barefoot on steep,

green knolls.

Collage of cloud and sky.

First Summer Storm

Skies lit up

       like fireworks.

Thunder roared

       like lions.

Trees danced in

       summer breezes.

Torrential rains

       blanketed highways.

Yearning for the

       serenity of home.

Summer's Swiftness

In a blink of an eye—

summer is gone.

Lengthy, carefree days

disappear like a dream.

Awakening to cool, autumn colors;

whimsical wind whispers.

Reality of winter-wildness—

solitary snow silence.

A Summer Afternoon

I ride a horse across a field.

The heat of the sun upon the steed.

A slight breeze caressing my face

as we speed past evergreen trees.

Passing geese by serene ponds.

Two fawns dance in the meadow.

Glimpsing crimson cardinals

in monumental oak trees.

Riding onto a rural path

leading to a nearby stream.

Life should be carefree

like a summer afternoon.

Haiku

Butterflies dancing

to the tunes of country music

on the radio.

.

Haiku (Moonglow on Ocean)

Moonglow on ocean.

Strollers wander along shores.

The beach at midnight.

Freedom

Freedom—

    butterfly wings

    soaring endless skies.

Freedom—

    scent of honeysuckle

    on June afternoons.

Freedom—

    innocence of childhood—

    eternal summer.

Promise of dawn

    newly beginning

    enchantment of life.

God's Perfect World

God has made

a perfect world

for humankind.

Respect this

splendid earth

with its variety of

floral jewels.

Be aware and care for

pristine waters

and forests.

Trying

Alleviating the pain of loneliness

in nursing home residents.

Bringing a smile to the faces

of forlorn children.

Providing food for

the homeless.

Making this world better

with all that love

can accomplish.

Thanks to the Creator

Thanks to the Creator

for the morning chorus

of cicadas;

the nocturnal chorale

of crickets.

Thanks to the Creator

for the radiance of rainbows;

the mystique of the ocean

sunrise splendor—sunset serenity.

Summer Lullaby

A porch morning filled with

the sound of cardinals.

Afternoon breezes at the beach.

Seagulls soar glistening sands.

Evenings filled with starlight.

The music of whimsical waves

lulling one to sleep.

Summer lullaby.

Memory

Memory is like writer's block.

The mind recalls what it wants

in its eager search for truth.

Forgetting the pain of broken dreams

the angst of the past.

Remembering the sweetness of life,

the warmth of hugs

childhood contentment.

Clinging to immortal youth,

promises of hope and peace.

Throughout the years, memory endures.

Memory keeps the joyful moments alive.

Azaleas

Ethereal floral display

Clusters of splendor

A symmetry of color

shimmering in sunlight.

Azaleas align verdant slopes

Pristine white, brilliant red

Amethyst plants nestled on

sea-green grass.

Between green pines and oaks

an effusion of blossoms

Graceful dogwoods surround

nature's vibrant jewels.

Life Is a Dusty Photograph

Life is a dusty photograph
Pictures collected
in musty albums
recall the
innocence of
childhood dreams.

The world appears
as a blur
in the realm
of the subconscious.

Events and milestones
are revealed
in the
recording of time.

Approaching Sixty

It always used to be the rage
   Women never discussed their age.
   Yet I have no reason to conceal
   my next birthday I will reveal.

I don't really feel near sixty at all
   although this past winter I had a fall.
   I had a broken wrist and elbow
   while slipping on the ice below.

I'm now looking at my life.
I'm a writer, mother and I've been a wife.
I have no idea what the future may hold.
But I will face new challenges as they
unfold.

Haiku

Loneliest at night.

Only music of insects.

Nature's lullaby.

Haiku

Birdfeeder swaying

on the slender branches of

the valiant dogwood.

Haiku

Lady Bird Johnson

created her legacy—

floral masterpiece.

Haiku

Washington, D.C.

capital of beauty

and allergies galore.

The Light of Dawn

The light of dawn

brightens the sky.

Birdsongs echo in

August air.

The light of dawn

shimmers on streams,

poplars, birches

and evergreens.

The light of dawn

fills the heart

with new beginnings

of hope and love.

God Is Forever

God is forever

   like eternal ocean waves

     birdsongs in dawnlight

       the rising and setting of the sun.

God is forever

   like the harmony of wind and sea

   a multitude of stars

     the ultimate universe.

After the Rain on a Summer Evening

Lightning and thunder cease.

Everything is clean and peaceful.

Between oak trees—

fireflies glow.

Humidity is gone for now.

Evening is cool and pleasing.

Laughter of children at the pool.

Everything is pure and pristine.

Nocturnal chorus of crickets.

The world in nightsong.

New Orleans

A city once so vibrant
    now filled with abandoned people
    searching for their loved ones
    through the mire.

Pets roam the streets
    without a home.
    Hungry and afraid
    children needing comfort.

There is hope as the nation
    sends food and water to the
    poorest of the poor
    trying to survive.

A better tomorrow is
    on the horizon;
    the compassion of humanity
    will prevail against despair.

August Days

In the backyard,

   dog escapes beneath the fence

      and runs around the lawn in a frenzy

Hummingbirds and Monarch butterflies

   darting between oak branches.

A miniature green frog

   leaps into verdant ivy.

The magnolia tree

   glistening in the sun.

Sipping pink lemonade

   in the shade

      on a steamy afternoon

I Am Content

I am content with God,
family and the miracle
of living.

I am pleased with
the floral splendor
of springtime,
summer's eternal ocean,
autumn's amazing array
of colors
and the quietude of winter.

I am blessed to witness
each sunrise
and the newness
of tomorrow.

Haiku

What noise is louder?

The roaring of the thunder

or the dog's snoring?

Freedom Is a Feeling

Freedom is a feeling
    of waking up
        without pain.

Freedom is a feeling
    of clean breezes
        caressing a sailboat
            in turquoise waves.

Freedom is a feeling of
    riding bareback
        across summer fields.

Freedom is a feeling
    of sleeping in
        dream serenity.

Haiku

In chill of winter

sparkling stars are far above

January trees.

The Odd Things in Life

Seagulls gliding above

a shopping mall.

Moon appearing in

afternoon sky.

Buds blooming in January

as if it were spring.

Dog walking owner—

keeping him fit and trim.

Cold

January winds roar

against the windows.

Geese fly in

silent, wide skies.

No flowers adorn

the frozen ground.

Animals are scarcely seen

in winter's brutal cold.

Haiku

Adorning the home

the majestic orchid is

floral masterpiece.

Writing a Poem

Writing a poem

in the quiet of home.

Rapidly, time disappears

as old age nears.

Although the future's unclear,

The dreams are still there.

God Makes It Right

When I feel uptight
  God makes it right.
  When I feel sad
  God makes me feel glad.

God comforts me
  when I'm lonely.
  When I'm worn out and tired
  God will get me inspired.

Sometimes, I feel like a fool
  but The Almighty does rule
  and will guide me
  on my life's journey.

God will always care
  when I'm in despair.
  I will always win
  with God, my companion.

Almost Midnight

Landscape lighting

glistening on grass

and newly trimmed

sculptured hedges.

Beneath the July sky,

majestic trees stand

in the stillness of

almost midnight.

Quiet

Quiet is a fawn

on the lawn at dawn.

Butterfly wings at

the hush of dusk.

A myriad of stars

brilliant in the midnight sky.

Squirrel (on a Fence)

A squirrel perched on a fence

gazing into the screened-in porch

where I sat on an old hammock chair

watching him eat acorns as

I had my spaghetti.

My dinner companion.

Haiku

Mother with young child

observes miles and miles of endless waves.

Eternal ocean.

Summer Dreamers

Dreaming of the beach
    the mystique of the ocean,
        aromatic salt air.

Lemonade afternoons
    on boardwalk benches.

Barefoot on the sand,
    walking along
        the sun-lit shores.

Dulcet breezes
    caressing green waves.

Soothing guitar music
    of summer dreamers.

Haiku (July Evening)

Sitting on the porch

listening to barking dogs

insect arias.

Beauty

The beauty of the soul
essence of the human;
tranquil and harmonious
like a serene song.

Natural beauty like
the splendor of the ocean,
the multitude of stars,
mountain, sea and sky.

The innocent beauty
of young children
in pristine fields
of butterflies.

The beauty of the mind
with purity of thought.
The beauty of the heart
creating love.

© Edna Searles 2008

Solitary Nights

Only the sound of crickets
permeating the solitude
of the country home.

No telephone disrupts
the calmness of evening
in a peaceful room.

Deer in a neighbor's yard
flees from the bright lights
of an approaching car.

The tranquil beauty
of vivid, pink roses
on solitary nights.

Backyard

Walking in the backyard,
  hearing the wind caressing
    green pines and blue spruces.

Watching the fireflies
  dancing in the air
    on summer evenings.

Observing a frog
  sitting still
    on the patio.

Topaz stars glisten
  in the nocturnal sky.

Haiku (A June Evening)

Wandering the yard

loud barking dogs are piercing

the silence of June.

Refreshing Spring

Sun on rhododendron.

Blue jays on dogwoods.

Cardinals songs amid

jasmine breezes.

A cloudless May sky.

Butterflies afloat

sylvan streams.

Refreshing spring.

The Colors of June

Sun streamed through the screened-in porch

glistening on vibrant red peonies

aligning verdant lawns.

Cardinals danced on sunlit branches.

Spring sunlight in honeysuckle woods.

The colors of June.

Tree Silhouettes

Tree silhouettes beneath the evening sky.

Topaz stars like nocturnal jewels.

Through the bay window

perceiving raccoon eyes.

Fawn and rabbit scamper

into the verdant forest.

Between the tree silhouettes,

a glimpse of a full moon.

Haiku

The sun does appear

and then it does disappear like

a fair-weather friend.

God's Goodness

God's goodness is seen

in the preciseness of waves

lulling one to sleep

in natural harmony.

God's goodness is reflected

in parents' precious love for children;

the nurturing they received in

their lives.

God's goodness is reflected

in the music of the soul

yearning to be close to

God's orchestra.

The Autumn Sky

Birds soar

upward toward

the autumn sky.

Cloud swirls

across the

horizon.

Squirrels perched

on oak branches

beneath the

surreal blueness.

Quintessential May

Sun brightness

streaming through

my window.

Spring melodies

echoing at dawn.

Robins dancing

on immaculate lawns.

Squirrels frolic

in forests.

Quintessential May.

Where Is Spring?

Snow is everywhere
    on trees, houses, streets and cars.
        Ice is pervasive
        on driveways, creeks, sidewalks and steps.

Where is spring?
    floral jewels in May,
        greening trees in April and
            budding branches in March?

Where is the sunshine
    on blooming dogwoods and cherry
        blossoms?

Where are the blue skies
        instead of perennial white skies
            filled with abundant snow?

Where is spring
    in never-ending,
        bitter cold winter?

Dancing Dog

He stands on his hind legs

and moves to the beat.

He dances on the patio

and is rewarded with a treat.

He moves so gracefully

and so precisely.

This little dog

is really in the groove.

Dancing dog, you are so spry.

Dancing dog, I can see why

you're so very cool

and you never even went to dancing school.

Spring Hat Returns

Spring hat returns

with vivid flowers

dogwoods, azaleas

and April showers.

Golden sunshine

in azure skies.

meadows filled

with butterflies.

Drinking freshly-squeezed

orange juice

beneath a majestic,

blue spruce.

Night's Quiet

Only sound
    in house
        hum of
           air conditioner.

Raindrops drum
    against windows.

Full moon
    glow in
        silent sky.

After frenzy
    of day,
        calmness of night.

Haiku

Through the car windows,

grandson, daughter and pet dog.

Three faces of love.

April Afternoon

April — white and pink dogwoods.

Slopes of golden daffodils.

Azaleas aligning

emerald yards.

Robins resting

on oak branches

beneath the tranquility

of a sea-blue sky.

Haiku (Reflections of Geese)

Reflections of geese

and towering evergreens

in serene waters.

Haiku *(Geese Crossing Street)*

Stopping all traffic

in the greening of springtime

geese crossing the street.

Haiku *(Daffodils)*

Daffodils in March

aligning green, steep incline

glittering at noon.

Sounds of Life

Rain on roof.

Horses hoof.

Songbirds at dawn.

Gardeners mow lawn.

Gulls glide over ocean.

Autumn leaves in motion.

Waterfalls in sunlight.

Baby cooing at night.

White Blankets

White blankets cover the earth tonight.

Mountains of snow glitter in starlight.

A jet plane is the only sound.

No animals are to be found.

Everybody's nestled in their cozy house.

People watching television with their spouse.

As the end of February is drawing near,

the miracle of spring is almost here.

God Is Everything

God controls the moon, wind and stars
   Venus, Pluto and Mars.
   God adores the smile on a baby's face
   and the entire human race.

God is compassionate and kind.
   In His love and caring, we can find,
   God is healing suffering
   in every human being.

God is everything
   summer, autumn, winter and spring
   are part of His natural plan
   as is His beloved creation—woman and man.

God is ever present in our dreams
   in the fields and streams
   every thought and song
   To God, does everything belong.

A Splendid Day

A splendid day
birches brighten
roadsides.

Butterflies flutter
in spring air.

Squirrels race
across the
wooden fence.

Geese glide
into azure skies.

Seagulls soar
above emerald waters.

Heavenly breezes
caressing
the verdant forest.

Purple-orange
sunset aglow

Other Books

Celebration
by Sherry Small Sundick ©1977
ISBN: 0-9707932-0-0

Rebirth
by Sherry Small Sundick ©1978
ISBN: 0-9707932-1-9

Potpourri
by Ruth Behrend Small and Sherry Small Sundick ©1978
ISBN: 0-9707932-2-7

Kaleidoscope
by Sherry Small Sundick ©1981
ISBN: 0-9707932-3-5

Choose Life
by Sherry Small Sundick ©1987
2nd Edition 2001, Illustrated by Edna Searles
ISBN: 0-9707932-4-3 / LCCC #2001126003

Sunrise
by Sherry Small Sundick ©1990
ISBN: 0-9707932-5-1

The Children's Alphabet Coloring Book
by Sherry Small Sundick ©1992
Illustrated by Edna Searles
ISBN: 0-9707932-6-X

Mind-Children
by Sherry Small Sundick ©1994
Illustrated by Edna Searles
ISBN: 0-9707932-7-8 / LCCC #94-93905

Mind-Travel
by Sherry Small Sundick ©1998
Illustrated by Edna Searles
ISBN: 0-9707932-8-6 / LCCC #98-067619

The Children's Animal Alphabet Coloring Book
by Sherry Small Sundick and Audrey Olberg ©2002
Illustrated by Edna Searles
ISBN: 0-9707932-9-4 / LCCC #2002095014

Creator and Creativity
by Sherry Small Sundick ©2004
Illustrated by Edna Searles
ISBN: 0-9745986-0-7 / LCCC #2003096747

The Children's Musical Alphabet Coloring Book
by Audrey Olberg and Sherry Small Sundick ©2006
Illustrated by Edna Searles
ISBN: 0-9745986-1-5 / LCCC #2006907583